DEVELOP YOUR EMOTIONAL INTELLIGENCE

*Techniques and Tools for
Achieving Personal Fulfillment*

Gisela M. Rentas, PhD

ISBN: 979-8-9922808-0-7

Produced by Publish Pros | publishpros.com

DEDICATION

To all those who seek to better understand themselves and others, to those who wish to transform their emotions into a source of power and growth. This book is for you, so that you can find the path to deeper well-being, a fuller life, and more authentic relationships, just as I have given myself this gift to live in a more emotionally intelligent way.

TABLE OF CONTENTS

INTRODUCTION

*"If you're reading this . . .
Congratulations, you're alive!"*

CHAD SUGG

Emotions are a state of mind characterized by an organic upheaval resulting from an external situation, which can manifest in gestures, laughter, or crying. In "Emotional Intelligence: Why it can matter more than IQ," Daniel Goleman indicates the etymology of the word "emotion" comes from "movere," the Latin verb meaning "to move."

On the other hand, other experts argue emotions are not just something we feel; they are a source of information. For example, the feeling of tiredness informs us about our energy or fatigue levels. Similarly, when we feel cold, it tells us about the temperature of the environment, and when we feel that someone is kind or trustworthy, the emotion is informing us about the level of friendship or affinity we have toward that person. Therefore, we think with emotions and must be cautious with the information we convey. For instance, when we infer emotions from tone of voice, music, literature, art, facial expressions, and body language, we also reason about the emotional consequences of our actions and our emotional state.

All emotions are, in essence, impulses to act. They are what make us move closer to or further from a particular person or situation. We make this inference because emotions help us understand our position and our relationship with the world and respond adaptively. This notion is the fundamental reason behind a view that considers emotions as motivating forces, adapting in a cognitive approach and, consequently, driving the development of the concept of emotional intelligence (EI).

OBJECTIVE OF THE BOOK

This book aims to be a guide to developing your emotional intelligence in a practical way. Through tools, exercises, and strategies, it will help you strengthen your self-awareness, improve your emotional management, and cultivate healthier, longer-lasting relationships. Emotional intelligence is not a fixed trait, but a skill that can be learned and perfected with practice and commitment.

CHAPTER 1: EMOTIONAL INTELLIGENCE (EI)

"Don't let the noise of others' opinions drown out your own inner voice. And, more importantly, have the courage to do what your heart and intuition tell you. Somehow, you already know what you truly want to become." – Daniel Goleman

In recent years, emotional intelligence (EI) has been studied more intensively due to findings in the literature. It has revealed that emotional intelligence can predict successful leadership and a fulfilling life. This has been one of the factors that has made the concept of EI a popular topic.

BRIEF HISTORY AND DEVELOPMENT OF EI

Although the term "emotional intelligence" is most commonly associated with psychologist Daniel Goleman, who was one of the scientists who focused on the concept of EI, the idea has roots in earlier psychological studies. Benjamin Palmer and Carlos Andújar indicate psychologists Peter Salovey and John Mayer introduced the term "emotional intelligence" in 1990, defining it as a form of intelligence that involves the ability to perceive, use, understand, and manage emotions effectively.

According to Andújar, Goleman was trained under the guidance of David McClelland, who had conducted studies on intelligence and questioned the role of intelligence tests in predicting success in life. Goleman mentioned that McClelland's research in the 1950s and 1960s led to the formulation of his theory on motivation, known as "the three needs"—power, achievement, and affiliation. Thus, Goleman expanded the concept by stating emotional intelligence was key not only for personal well-being but also for professional and social success. Since then, EI has become an important area of study in psychology, education, and business management.

WHAT IS EMOTIONAL INTELLIGENCE?

For Goleman, emotional intelligence is "the ability to recognize our own feelings and those of others, to motivate ourselves, and to manage emotions in ourselves and in our relationships with others." Freytes interpreted this definition as a set of skills, attitudes, abilities, and competencies that determine an individual's behavior, reactions, and mental states, among others. Salovey and Mayer defined EI as "the ability to perceive and express emotions, assimilate our thoughts emotionally, understand and reason about emotions, and regulate our emotions and those of others." For Andújar, this definition is a form of social intelligence that involves the ability to monitor one's own feelings and emotions, discriminate between them, and use this information to guide thoughts and actions.

Unlike IQ (intelligence quotient), which measures cognitive abilities, and, according to Goleman, contributes only twenty percent to the factors that determine success in life, EI focuses on emotional and social skills such as self-awareness, self-control, empathy, motivation, and interpersonal relationships. These skills allow greater control over our emotional reactions and help build more meaningful and successful relationships.

DIFFERENCE BETWEEN EMOTIONAL INTELLIGENCE (EI) AND INTELLIGENCE QUOTIENT (IQ)

While traditional intelligence (IQ) has long been the standard for measuring a person's "mental capacity," it is not always a reliable predictor of personal or professional success. McClelland questioned the ". . . false but widespread belief that success depends solely on intellectual ability . . . ." Among the criteria he proposed was that ". . . traditional academic skills such as grades and degrees do not allow us to adequately predict job performance or success in life . . . ."

Instead, he proposed that the traits differentiating the most outstanding workers from those who simply perform well should be sought in competencies such as empathy, self-discipline, and discipline. EI complements IQ by focusing on skills that enable effective interaction and communication with oneself and others. While IQ is a relatively fixed trait, EI can be developed and improved throughout life.

WHY IS EMOTIONAL INTELLIGENCE (EI) IMPORTANT?

In everyday life, we face constant emotional challenges: work stress, personal relationships, goals, and failures. EI helps us cope with these challenges in a more conscious and adaptive way. Various studies have shown people with a high level of EI tend to have better mental health, greater job satisfaction, and more harmonious personal relationships. It is also a key factor for effective leadership and teamwork in professional contexts.

Emotional intelligence is more important than cognitive intelligence because, to succeed in life, one must not only possess knowledge in various areas of learning, but also have the ability to relate positively to others, enjoy notable self-esteem, have the drive to overcome difficulties, value people, not be discouraged by failures, and develop the will and character to reject all kinds of temptations. Emotions are essential for human beings, because through them we give meaning to people and to our own being. Intelligence is tested not only in numbers but in the complex variety of situations and challenges life presents.

HOW DOES EI INFLUENCE OUR LIVES?

- **In the personal realm:** EI helps us become more aware of our emotions, recognize our behavioral patterns, and make decisions that promote our well-being. It also improves how we respond to stress and deal with failures.

- **In interpersonal relationships:** Empathy and social skills strengthen our relationships by enabling us to understand and respond to others' needs. EI helps build deep and meaningful connections, essential for developing stable and supportive relationships.

- **In the professional realm:** EI is fundamental in leadership and teamwork. An emotionally intelligent leader can inspire, motivate, and guide their collaborators, while a team with high EI handles conflicts better and collaborates more effectively.

COMPONENTS OF EMOTIONAL INTELLIGENCE

Emotional intelligence (EI) can be divided into five main components:

1. **Self-awareness:** The knowledge of oneself, our emotions, thoughts, and values. People with high self-awareness are able to recognize how their emotions influence their decisions and actions.

2. **Self-regulation:** The ability to manage impulsive emotions and respond appropriately in difficult situations. Self-regulation helps one to maintain calm and act rationally rather than being overwhelmed by intense emotions.

3. **Motivation:** Emotionally intelligent people tend to be motivated from within, which allows them to set and achieve goals with perseverance and optimism, even in the face of obstacles.

4. **Empathy:** The ability to understand and feel what others are emotionally experiencing. It is essential for building healthy interpersonal relationships and connecting deeply with others.

5. **Social skills:** These skills allow effective management of relationships, clear communication, conflict resolution, and constructive collaboration.

In the upcoming chapters, we will explain each of these components in more detail.

NOTES:

CHAPTER 2: UNDERSTANDING SELF-AWARENESS

"What is needed to change a person is to change their self-awareness."

ABRAHAM MASLOW

WHAT IS SELF-AWARENESS?

Self-awareness is the first pillar of emotional intelligence. It is the ability to recognize and understand our emotions, thoughts, motivations, and how they influence our behavior. Being aware of our emotions as they arise, and how they affect our actions and decisions, allows us to live more intentionally, responding rather than reacting impulsively.

Developing self-awareness means observing our emotional states and thought patterns without judging them or trying to change them immediately. It is about accepting our emotions, both positive and negative, and understanding each one serves a purpose.

WHY IS SELF-AWARENESS IMPORTANT?

Self-awareness is essential because it allows us to:

- **Make better decisions:** When we are aware of our emotions, we avoid acting impulsively or irrationally.

- **Improve our relationships:** By recognizing how our emotions affect our interactions, we can communicate more openly and authentically.

- **Promote personal growth:** Self-awareness helps us identify areas for improvement and actively work on them.

HOW SELF-AWARENESS WORKS: LEVELS OF AWARENESS

Self-awareness has different levels, including emotional recognition, awareness of patterns, understanding our values and motivations, and deep self-knowledge. These levels are interconnected and complement each other.

Emotional recognition. This is the first step and involves identifying and naming our emotions. Knowing if we are sad, angry, frustrated, or happy is essential to managing how we respond.

Awareness of patterns. Self-awareness also involves recognizing emotional and behavioral patterns. Are there specific situations that trigger certain emotions in us? How do we typically react to pressure or criticism?

Understanding values and motivations. This level of self-awareness allows us to understand why certain goals are important to us and what our core values are. Being aware of our internal motivations helps us make decisions aligned with our purpose and prevents us from being swayed by external pressures.

Deep self-knowledge. The deepest level of self-awareness is recognizing and accepting our strengths, weaknesses, limitations, and aspirations. This knowledge helps us be compassionate with ourselves and accept that, like everyone else, we are a "work in progress."

STRATEGIES TO DEVELOP SELF-AWARENESS

1. **Practice self-reflection:** Dedicate a few minutes at the end of the day to reflect on your emotions and behaviors. This habit of reflection will help you identify patterns. Ask yourself:

   - How did I feel today?
   - Why did I react that way in certain situations?
   - What were the predominant emotions I experienced?

2. **Reflective writing (journaling):** Writing about our experiences and emotions can be a powerful tool for developing self-awareness. Try keeping a journal where you record your emotions and thoughts of the day. Over time, you will be able to spot trends and better understand how certain events affect you.

3. **Mindfulness and meditation:** Mindfulness involves observing our thoughts and emotions without judging them. Through meditation, we can train ourselves to be aware of the present moment and accept our emotions as they are. These practices promote self-awareness by helping us recognize our emotions as they occur.

4. **Accept feedback:** Receiving honest feedback from friends, family, or colleagues can provide valuable insight into how others perceive

us. Sometimes, others notice behavioral patterns we don't perceive. Feedback helps us become more aware of how our emotions and actions affect those around us.

5. **Identify emotional triggers:** An emotional trigger is a situation or event that causes an intense emotional reaction. To develop self-awareness, it is important to recognize these triggers and understand their origin. Ask yourself which situations tend to trigger certain emotions in you and analyze the underlying causes.

6. **Create an emotional map:** Identify your most common emotions and connect each one with the situations, people, or places that generate them. This helps visualize patterns and better understand your emotional reactions.

PRACTICAL EXERCISES FOR SELF-AWARENESS

1. **The "3 Questions" exercise:** At the end of the day, answer:

   - What emotions did I feel today?
   - What situations triggered these emotions?
   - How would I like to respond the next time I feel this way?

2. **The "Wheel of Emotions" exercise:** This wheel refers to a visual tool used in psychology and education to help individuals identify and express their emotions. The wheel consists of various segments, each representing different emotional states or feelings. Instead of simply saying you feel "bad" or "good," identify whether you are joyful, amazed, angry, sad, scared, frustrated, etc. This distinction helps you better understand what you're feeling by promoting emotional literacy and self-reflection, making it easier for people to navigate and express their emotional experiences.

3. **Writing letters to your emotions:** Sometimes, we can gain more clarity by writing as if we were directly addressing a specific emotion. For example, write a letter to your "anxiety" or your "joy" and describe how it makes you feel, when it typically appears, and how it affects your life.

HOW SELF-AWARENESS TRANSFORMS OUR LIVES

When we cultivate self-awareness, we not only make decisions that align with our values, we also build a healthier relationship with ourselves. We become more patient, less critical, and more understanding by recognizing our emotions are temporary and we can consciously manage them.

Self-awareness also allows us to communicate more authentically with others, as we know how to express what we feel without suppressing it or reacting impulsively. This strengthens both our personal and professional relationships because people appreciate and trust those who communicate with transparency and empathy.

Developing self-awareness is a continuous process that requires time and practice. It is not about reaching a goal but about constantly learning about ourselves and accepting our emotions as part of the human experience.

CONCLUSION

In essence, self-awareness is the foundation for personal growth and meaningful connections. By understanding ourselves better, we not only improve how we navigate our own emotions but also how we engage with others. As we grow in self-awareness, we begin to lead lives that are more aligned with our values, fostering healthy relationships and a greater sense of inner peace. While the journey may be ongoing, each step we take toward greater self-awareness enhances our ability to live authentically, with compassion for ourselves and others. This transformative process empowers us to approach life with clarity, confidence, and emotional resilience.

NOTES:

CHAPTER 3: PRACTICING SELF-CONTROL

"Self-control is strength. Right thought is mastery.
Calmness is power."

JAMES ALLEN

WHAT IS SELF-CONTROL?

Self-control is the ability to manage our emotions, impulses, and behaviors, especially in difficult or stressful situations. According to Goleman, it is the "component of emotional intelligence that frees us from being prisoners of our feelings." It is the skill that allows us to respond consciously and appropriately rather than reacting impulsively. Practicing self-control does not mean repressing or ignoring our emotions, but rather learning to channel them in a constructive way.

Self-control is especially important when facing conflicts, challenges, or temptations that may divert us from our goals. In the article, "Self-Control," by Allen García, it is mentioned that people with high self-control are able to master their thoughts and actions, which can be beneficial in many situations. It enables us to act in a way that is consistent with our values and objectives, instead of being carried away by the emotions that arise in the moment.

WHY IS SELF-CONTROL IMPORTANT?

Self-control allows us to:

- **Make thoughtful decisions:** By not acting impulsively, we avoid decisions we might regret later.

- **Reduce stress and frustration:** By maintaining calm and controlling our emotional response in tense situations, we help preserve a positive attitude and avoid emotional burnout.

- **Improve our relationships:** Self-control is essential for managing conflicts and maintaining respectful and empathetic communication.

- **Achieve long-term goals:** By resisting impulses that distract us from our objectives, we stay on track toward what we truly want.

COMPONENTS OF SELF-CONTROL

Recognition of impulse: The first step in developing self-control is recognizing when an emotional impulse arises, such as anger or frustration. Being aware of these impulses in the moment allows us to pause and choose how we want to respond.

Emotional regulation: Once we recognize an impulse, we can regulate the emotion so it does not dominate our actions. Emotional regulation enables us to calm our emotions and avoid automatic reactions.

Persistence and resilience: Self-control also involves staying focused on our goals, despite distractions or obstacles. This requires patience and the ability to tolerate discomfort without giving in.

Conscious decision-making: Finally, self-control allows us to evaluate the potential consequences of our actions before we act. Making decisions based on our goals and values rather than giving in to momentary impulses is key to exercising self-control.

STRATEGIES TO DEVELOP SELF-CONTROL

1. **Practice deep breathing and mindfulness:** In tense moments, practicing deep breathing techniques can help reduce emotional reactivity. Breathe slowly, inhale through your nose, and exhale through your mouth. This helps calm the nervous system and regain control.

2. **Take a pause (10-Second Rule):** Before reacting in a stressful situation, count to ten slowly or step away for a moment if possible. This brief pause helps reduce emotional intensity and allows you to think before acting.

3. **Visualize the consequences:** Visualize the outcomes of acting impulsively versus responding consciously. Ask yourself, "What will happen if I act this way? How will I feel afterward?" Remembering the potential consequences helps us to make decisions that align with our goals and values.

4. **Set emotional boundaries:** Identify your emotional boundaries and learn to recognize when it's necessary to distance yourself from certain situations or people that may trigger intense emotions. Boundaries help protect our peace of mind and prevent situations that overwhelm us.

5. **Practice in low-stress situations:** Practicing self-control in low-pressure situations (e.g., in a long line or when something goes

wrong in your daily routine) helps prepare us to respond in more challenging situations.

6. **Reduce distractions:** Often, the lack of self-control arises from distractions or impulsivity. Reduce distractions that hinder your concentration on important activities (e.g., turning off phone notifications or creating a distraction-free workspace).

7. **Use positive affirmations:** When you feel like you're losing control, use positive affirmations like "I can handle this situation calmly," or "I choose to respond rather than react." These affirmations help reinforce your self-control capacity and maintain a centered mindset.

EXERCISES TO DEVELOP SELF-CONTROL

1. **Impulse journal:** Keep a record of situations where you experience an intense emotion that urges you to act impulsively. Write down what emotion you felt, what your first impulse was, and how you ultimately chose to act. Reflect on what you could do differently next time to improve your response.

2. **The "Two-Minute" exercise:** When you feel the urge to act immediately, wait two minutes before doing so. Use that time to think about the possible consequences of your action and decide if it's the best choice. With practice, you can extend this waiting time to five or ten minutes.

3. **Practice delayed gratification:** Exercises in delayed gratification, such as waiting before rewarding yourself with a treat or a reward, increase your ability to resist impulses and strengthen self-control.

Every time you choose to wait before satisfying an immediate need, you reinforce this skill.

4. **Simulate challenging scenarios:** Visualize situations where you tend to lose self-control and rehearse how you would like to respond in those cases. Imagine staying calm, using your self-control strategies, and making conscious decisions. This mental practice will help you respond effectively when those situations arise in real life.

5. **Replace negative impulses with healthy alternatives:** If you tend to engage in habits like emotional eating or procrastination to manage intense emotions, identify alternative, more constructive activities. You can go for a walk, exercise, journal, or listen to music. Replacing impulsive responses with healthier alternatives is an excellent self-control exercise.

HOW SELF-CONTROL IMPROVES OUR RELATIONSHIPS AND WELL-BEING

Practicing self-control deeply impacts our personal and professional relationships. It helps us avoid unnecessary conflicts, listen actively, and respond with empathy, even in challenging situations. Furthermore, it enhances our self-esteem as we learn to trust our ability to manage our emotions and act according to our values.

Self-control is also crucial for personal well-being. By better managing our emotional responses, we reduce stress and become more resilient in the face of difficulties. It allows us to act consistently with our goals, preventing momentary emotions from steering us away from what we truly want to achieve.

CONCLUSION

Self-control is an essential skill that can be developed with practice and dedication. It is not about repressing our emotions but learning to recognize them and respond consciously. Over time, this emotional regulation will enable us to live more intentionally, improve our relationships, and move toward our personal and professional goals with determination and patience.

NOTES:

CHAPTER 4: INTERNAL MOTIVATION

"Energy and persistence conquer all things."

BENJAMIN FRANKLIN

WHAT IS INTERNAL MOTIVATION?

Internal motivation, also known as intrinsic motivation, is the force that drives us to act and achieve our goals from a genuine and deep desire. As Goleman states, "the key word is achievement." Unlike external motivation, which is driven by rewards or external recognition, internal motivation comes from our own interests, passions, values, and personal purpose.

When we are internally motivated, our actions feel meaningful and aligned with our essence. Internal motivation is crucial for the development of emotional intelligence, as it allows us to stay focused and committed to achieving our goals, even in the face of challenges and obstacles.

WHY IS INTERNAL MOTIVATION IMPORTANT?

Internal motivation has several important benefits:

- **Encourages perseverance:** People with internal motivation tend to be more persistent because they are driven by something beyond external rewards.

- **Increases well-being:** When we do things we are passionate about, our satisfaction and sense of purpose increase, contributing to our emotional well-being.

- **Promotes personal growth:** Internal motivation drives us to continually improve and explore new development opportunities.

- **Generates greater resilience:** Being motivated from within helps us overcome failures and adapt to changes, as our commitment to our goals is deeper and less dependent on immediate results.

TYPES OF MOTIVATION

Motivation can be divided into two main types:

Intrinsic motivation (internal). This arises from a personal interest or enjoyment of the activity itself. It is when you do something because it brings satisfaction, learning, or growth. For example, reading a book because you love the subject or learning a skill for the joy of knowing more.

Extrinsic motivation (external). This is the drive to act in order to obtain an external reward or avoid a negative consequence. For example, working only for the paycheck or studying solely to pass an exam. While extrinsic motivation can be effective in the short term, it tends to be less sustainable in the long run.

DISCOVERING YOUR INTERNAL MOTIVATION

1. **Identify your personal values:** Values are principles or beliefs that guide our decisions and actions. Ask yourself: "What is most important to me in life? What values can I not compromise?" These values may include authenticity, continuous learning, compassion, or creativity. Connecting your goals and actions to your values will help sustain your internal motivation.

2. **Find your purpose:** Having a purpose gives us direction and meaning. Think about the impact you want to have on the world, your community, or your personal environment. Reflect on how your skills and passions can contribute to something bigger than yourself. A strong purpose is an inexhaustible source of motivation.

3. **Connect with your passions:** Passion is one of the most powerful forces that motivates us from within. Reflect on the activities that make you lose track of time and you enjoy doing, regardless of whether others value them. Incorporating more of these activities into your life can nourish your internal motivation.

4. **Define your personal goals:** Internal goals, those that are aligned with our deep desires and values, are a great source of motivation. Rather than focusing on what others expect from you, set goals that truly inspire you and are connected to who you are and who you want to be.

STRATEGIES TO FOSTER INTERNAL MOTIVATION

1. **Develop a growth mindset:** The growth mindset is the belief that our skills and talents can be developed through effort, learning, and perseverance. This mindset helps you see challenges as

opportunities for growth rather than obstacles, strengthening your internal motivation.

2. **Set small and meaningful goals:** Large goals can feel overwhelming and demotivating. Break them down into smaller steps and celebrate your achievements along the way. This will allow you to experience a sense of progress and motivate you to keep going.

3. **Find satisfaction in the process, not just in the result:** When you focus solely on the end results, you miss the opportunity to enjoy the process. Find gratification in learning and in the small daily achievements. Each step you take toward your goals is a victory in itself.

4. **Use self-reflection to stay focused:** Take time regularly to reflect on your goals and progress. Ask yourself if the activities and decisions you are making are bringing you closer to your objectives and values. Self-reflection strengthens commitment and allows you to adjust your efforts according to your purpose.

5. **Surround yourself with people who share your passion:** The people around you influence your motivation. Surround yourself with people who share similar interests and who inspire you to keep growing. Connections with motivated people can revitalize your own commitment and enthusiasm.

6. **Accept and learn from failures:** Mistakes and failures are inevitable in any growth process. Instead of becoming demotivated, use them as learning opportunities. Reflect on what you can improve and how you can face challenges with more strength in the future.

EXERCISES TO DEVELOP INTERNAL MOTIVATION

1. **The "5 Whys" exercise:** When you have a goal, ask yourself, "Why do I want to achieve this?" and answer honestly. Then, to each answer, ask again, "Why?" Repeat this five times. This exercise helps you discover the true reason behind your goals and connects you with your internal motivation.

2. **Create a personal vision map:** Create a visual map of your dreams, values, and goals. You can include images, keywords, or inspirational phrases that represent your desires and aspirations. This visual map will constantly remind you of the "why" behind your efforts and help keep you motivated.

3. **Weekly reflection:** Dedicate a moment each week to reflect on your progress. Ask yourself: "What achievements did I make this week? What obstacles did I face, and how did I overcome them?" This habit strengthens your internal motivation by recognizing progress and learning from challenges.

4. **Write a letter to your future self:** Imagine you are the person you want to be in five or ten years. Write a letter to your current self, motivating and reminding yourself why it's worth putting in the effort today. This letter will help you visualize your future and maintain commitment to your goals.

5. **Establish a life manifesto:** Write a brief manifesto that reflects your values, goals, and what you hope to achieve in life. Review this manifesto regularly and use it as a guide in moments of doubt or demotivation. Having a personal "north" will strengthen your motivation and remind you of the purpose behind your efforts.

HOW INTERNAL MOTIVATION TRANSFORMS OUR LIFE

When we develop motivation from within, our actions become more meaningful and aligned with our essence. We become less dependent on external validation and more focused on what truly matters to us. Internal motivation allows us to enjoy the journey toward our goals and face challenges with a resilient attitude.

Furthermore, motivation from within promotes personal growth and emotional well-being, as our decisions are guided by a genuine desire to be our best selves. When we are driven by internal motivation, we radiate authenticity and passion, which also inspires those around us.

CONCLUSION

Internal motivation is a powerful and lasting source of energy to help us achieve our goals. By connecting with our values, passions, and purpose, we develop motivation that sustains us in difficult moments and fills us with satisfaction in success. Practicing internal motivation is an act of self-awareness and commitment to our best version, and it is an essential component for living a full and purposeful life.

NOTES:

CHAPTER 5: EMPATHY AND UNDERSTANDING OTHERS

"Empathy is the medicine the world needs."

ANONYMOUS

WHAT IS EMPATHY?

Empathy is the ability to understand and share the feelings of others. It is a fundamental skill of emotional intelligence and is the one that is "most easily recognized"—according to Goleman— as it allows us to connect emotionally with others, understand their perspective, and respond compassionately. Being empathetic does not only mean "walking in someone else's shoes," but also being able to feel and understand what another person experiences from their point of view.

WHY IS EMPATHY IMPORTANT?

Empathy has numerous benefits both personally and in our relationships:

- **Strengthens relationships:** Empathy facilitates connection and mutual understanding, which improves the quality of our interpersonal relationships.

- **Increases compassion and patience:** By understanding what others feel, we become more patient and compassionate toward their struggles.

- **Facilitates conflict resolution:** Empathy helps us view problems from others' perspectives, making conflict resolution easier and allowing us to avoid misunderstandings.

- **Improves leadership:** Empathetic leaders are better able to motivate and understand their teams, fostering a culture of respect and collaboration.

- **Promotes emotional well-being:** Connecting deeply with others makes us feel more supported and understood, which enhances our emotional well-being.

TYPES OF EMPATHY

Cognitive empathy. This is the ability to understand another person's point of view or thoughts, without necessarily feeling what they feel. This type of empathy allows us to recognize the thoughts and feelings of others rationally.

Emotional or affective empathy. This is the capacity to share another person's feelings and feel an emotional connection with them. This type of empathy enables us to experience others' emotions and respond more compassionately and sensitively.

Both types of empathy are important and complementary, as together they allow us to build deeper, more satisfying relationships and improve our ability to resolve conflicts and understand others.

BARRIERS TO DEVELOPING EMPATHY

Although empathy is a natural skill, there are obstacles that can hinder its development:

1. **Lack of mindfulness.** In a society full of distractions, it's easy to be physically present but not truly pay attention to others.

2. **Judgments and prejudices.** Judging or labeling someone limits our ability to understand their perspective and emotions.

3. **Ego and lack of self-awareness.** When we are overly focused on our own needs and problems, it is hard to connect with how others feel.

4. **Fear of intense emotions.** Some people avoid connecting deeply with others due to the fear of experiencing uncomfortable or painful emotions.

5. **Cultural ignorance or differences.** Culture can influence how people express and understand emotions. Sometimes, cultural barriers make it difficult to understand the feelings of those with a different perspective.

STRATEGIES FOR CULTIVATING EMPATHY

1. **Listen actively:** Empathy begins with the ability to truly listen to others. Active listening involves giving full attention, not interrupting or judging, and showing interest through gestures and facial expressions. Ask open-ended questions and avoid distractions while the other person is speaking.

2. **Observe non-verbal language:** Much of emotional communication occurs through body language, facial expression, and tone of voice. Practicing observing these cues helps capture emotions that may not be expressed in words.

3. **Practice emotional validation:** Validation is the act of acknowledging the other person's feelings without judgment. Sometimes, a simple "I understand how you feel," or "I can see this is hard for you," can make the other person feel heard and understood.

4. **Genuinely care about others:** Show a genuine interest in the experiences and perspectives of others. Ask about their opinions, listen to their stories, and seek to learn from their experiences. When you develop sincere curiosity, empathy emerges naturally.

5. **Practice alternate perspectives:** Try to see situations from the other person's point of view. Ask yourself, "How would this person feel in this situation? What might they be thinking?" This exercise helps expand your understanding and prevents hasty judgments.

6. **Manage your own prejudices:** Identify and work to overcome prejudices that might hinder your ability to empathize with certain groups or individuals. By setting aside these biases, you can relate to others in a more open and understanding way.

7. **Recall personal similar experiences:** When someone is going through a tough time, remembering a moment when you felt similarly can help you better understand their emotions. Even if you haven't experienced the exact same situation, connecting with your own emotions allows you to approach the situation with more compassion.

EXERCISES TO DEVELOP EMPATHY

1. **Empathy journal:** Keep a journal where you write about the interactions you had during the day and reflect on the emotions of the people you encountered. Ask yourself, "How did I feel? What emotions or needs might have been behind their words?" This exercise strengthens your ability to reflect and understand others.

2. **Practice mirror listening:** In a conversation, listen actively and repeat, in your own words, what the other person expressed. This exercise helps ensure you truly understand what the other person is feeling and thinking and also shows them you've accurately received their message.

3. **Role-playing:** Put yourself in the other person's shoes and act as if you were them, thinking about how you would respond to different situations from their perspective. This exercise is especially useful for developing cognitive empathy and seeing how you might react if you were in their position.

4. **Gratitude and appreciation:** At the end of each day, make a list of the people who positively impacted your day and note the value of those interactions. Expressing gratitude toward the people in your life helps you appreciate them more and become more empathetic toward them.

5. **Mindfulness:** Practicing mindfulness or full meditation helps you be present and calms your mind, which facilitates deep listening and greater sensitivity toward others. With a calm mind, it is easier to pay true attention to others' emotions and connect with them without distractions.

HOW EMPATHY IMPROVES OUR RELATIONSHIPS AND WELL-BEING

Empathy is a powerful skill that transforms our relationships by improving the quality of our interactions and promoting an environment of respect and understanding. As Goleman states, "People who have it can distinguish the subtleties of body language, and they can pick up the message that lies behind the words." Therefore, when we are empathetic, people around us feel valued and heard, which strengthens our bonds and creates open and sincere communication.

Additionally, empathy not only benefits others, but also has a positive impact on our own well-being. By connecting with the emotions of others, we develop greater compassion, which in turn reduces feelings of loneliness and isolation. Empathy also helps us influence others' actions, resolve conflicts peacefully, lead effectively, and see the world from a broader perspective, fostering an attitude of tolerance and respect for differences.

CONCLUSION

Empathy is the bridge that connects us with others on a deep and meaningful level. Through empathy, we can understand and respect the diversity of human experiences, which enriches our relationships and strengthens our emotional intelligence. Practicing empathy not only allows us to be better friends, colleagues, partners, and family members, but also enriches our lives by allowing us to see the world from a variety of perspectives and build relationships based on mutual understanding and compassion.

NOTES:

CHAPTER 6: SOCIAL SKILLS AND INTERPERSONAL RELATIONSHIPS

*"You don't have to dim someone else's light
to make yours shine."*

GANDHI

WHAT ARE SOCIAL SKILLS?

Social skills are a set of abilities that allow us to interact effectively, respectfully, and harmoniously with others. As Goleman points out, "they are not as simple as they seem." These skills encompass a range of behaviors expressed in interactions with others, allowing for the appropriate expression of feelings, attitudes, desires, opinions, and rights according to the context, enabling us to defend our rights while respecting the rights of others.

Social skills include a range of habits, from the ability to start and maintain a conversation, to more complex skills such as negotiation, conflict management, and building support networks. These skills are essential for developing healthy and positive interpersonal relationships, as they help us understand others and build meaningful and lasting connections.

In the context of emotional intelligence, social skills go beyond simply being "likable" or extroverted; they are fundamental in creating a supportive, collaborative, and respectful environment. People with highly developed social skills often stand out due to their conciliatory and approachable character. Developing these skills not only improves our quality of life but also makes us more empathetic, understanding, and effective in our personal and professional relationships.

WHY ARE SOCIAL SKILLS IMPORTANT?

Social skills play a crucial role in many aspects of life:

- **Facilitate effective communication:** Expressing and understanding others clearly helps reduce misunderstandings and strengthen connections.

- **Encourage cooperation:** People with strong social skills are typically better at teamwork and conflict resolution, which makes it easier to achieve common goals.

- **Increase emotional well-being:** Healthy and constructive relationships reduce stress and loneliness and improve life satisfaction.

- **Contribute to professional success:** Interpersonal skills are highly valued in the workplace as good relationship management facilitates leadership, negotiation, and collaboration.

- **Promote resilience:** Strong relationships provide an emotional support system, helping us cope with challenges more effectively.

FACTORS OF SOCIAL SKILLS

Effective communication. The ability to express our ideas, needs, and feelings clearly and assertively is fundamental. It includes both verbal communication (what we say) and non-verbal communication (body language, tone of voice, and facial expressions). Effective communication allows us to express ourselves without ambiguity and to actively listen to others.

Assertiveness. Being assertive means expressing our opinions and desires clearly and respectfully without being aggressive or submitting to others' desires. Assertiveness helps establish healthy boundaries and defend our needs without resorting to aggression or passivity.

Conflict resolution. Conflicts are inevitable in any relationship. The ability to address them constructively, without avoiding issues or reacting explosively, is essential. Conflict resolution involves finding solutions that benefit both parties while maintaining calm and respect throughout the process.

Active listening. Active listening means giving full attention to the speaker, showing interest and understanding. It involves responding with gestures, questions, or statements that indicate we understand their message. This type of listening fosters empathy and helps create a genuine connection with others.

Adaptability. Relationships require flexibility and the ability to adapt to different situations and people. Adaptability involves being able to accept change, adjust to various communication styles, and find ways to connect in different contexts.

Cooperation and teamwork. This skill involves working with others to achieve a common goal while respecting the ideas and contributions of others. Cooperation is based on empathy, respect, and a willingness to help and collaborate.

Ability to give and receive feedback. Feedback is an important tool for personal and professional growth. Knowing how to give constructive feedback and receive criticism positively is essential for improving and learning from our experiences.

Establishing healthy boundaries. Knowing when to say "no" and setting boundaries in our relationships is crucial for maintaining emotional health. Clear boundaries help us take care of our well-being and establish more respectful and balanced relationships.

STRATEGIES TO DEVELOP SOCIAL SKILLS

1. **Practice self-observation:** Take time to reflect on how you behave in social interactions. Do you listen actively or tend to interrupt? Are you assertive or do you struggle to express your opinions? Self-observation is key to identifying areas for improvement.

2. **Improve your non-verbal communication:** Pay attention to your body language, facial expressions, and tone of voice. Non-verbal communication represents a significant portion of the message we convey, and improving it can make a big difference in how others perceive us.

3. **Use the "I" technique in assertive communication:** Instead of blaming others or making accusatory statements, express your feelings using the "I" technique. For example, instead of saying, "You're always late," you could say, "I feel frustrated when you're late because I really value our time together." This technique helps

communicate your needs without making the other person feel attacked.

4. **Practice active listening:** Consciously try to listen without interrupting. Respond with affirmations such as "I understand," "That sounds difficult," or "Thank you for sharing that with me." Active listening requires focusing and putting distractions aside to be present in the conversation.

5. **Show empathy:** Try to understand others' feelings and perspectives. Empathy is the foundation of emotional connection and allows you to respond more sensitively and compassionately.

6. **Establish healthy boundaries:** Practice saying "no" when necessary and setting clear boundaries in your relationships. Boundaries not only protect you emotionally, but also establish clear expectations and foster mutual respect.

7. **Seek opportunities to practice:** Engage in activities that allow you to improve your social skills, such as working in teams, attending social events, or joining clubs or interest groups. The more you practice, the more comfortable these interactions will become.

8. **Receive constructive feedback:** If someone offers you criticism, try to listen without becoming defensive. Reflect on what you can learn from it and how you can improve. Feedback is an opportunity to grow, and accepting it with humility is a sign of emotional maturity.

EXERCISES TO STRENGTHEN SOCIAL SKILLS

1. **Role-playing:** Practice social situations with friends or colleagues to develop your skills. You can simulate a situation where you need to be assertive or resolve a conflict. Role-playing is an excellent way to practice before facing real-life situations.

2. **Observe people with strong social skills:** Watch how people with good interpersonal skills behave. Pay attention to their body language, how they listen and respond to others, and how they manage interactions. You can learn a lot by observing others.

3. **Write a list of personal boundaries:** Reflect on the boundaries you need to protect your well-being and relationships. Make a list of those boundaries and share it with those closest to you if necessary. This will help you practice setting clear and respectful boundaries.

4. **Constructive feedback exercise:** Find a trusted person and ask them to give you feedback on your communication, listening, or collaboration skills. Practice receiving this feedback calmly and reflect on the areas for improvement.

5. **Social interaction journal:** Keep a record of significant social interactions each day. Reflect on what went well, what you could have done differently, and set goals for improving future interactions.

6. **Try the "mindful pause":** Before responding in a conversation, take a brief pause to think about what you are going to say. This gives you time to organize your thoughts and respond thoughtfully, rather than reacting impulsively.

HOW SOCIAL SKILLS IMPROVE OUR LIVES AND RELATIONSHIPS

Social skills enable us to build more meaningful and lasting relationships. They are behaviors, patterns of thinking, emotions, and actions that make it easier for us to interact in ways that maximize benefits and minimize negative repercussions, both short and long term. When we can express our thoughts and emotions effectively, listen actively to others, and approach conflicts with respect, our relationships become more fulfilling and harmonious. Interpersonal skills also help us understand others, fostering greater empathy and cooperation.

In the professional realm, social skills make us more effective collaborators and leaders, facilitating communication, teamwork, and the achievement of common goals. As Goleman states, "empathy with purpose." Moreover, having strong social skills contributes to our emotional well-being by enabling us to create strong and healthy support networks.

CONCLUSION

Developing social skills is an investment in our relationships and personal growth. As we practice effective communication, active listening, assertiveness, and conflict resolution, our interactions become more genuine and fulfilling. Social skills are the foundation of complete emotional intelligence, allowing us to connect effectively with others.

NOTES:

CHAPTER 7: APPLYING EMOTIONAL INTELLIGENCE IN WORK AND LIFE

"Change your focus, and you will change your emotions. Change your emotion, and your focus will change places."

FREDERICK DODSON

INTRODUCTION

Emotional intelligence (EI) is a powerful skill that, when applied practically, can significantly improve the quality of our personal and professional lives. The first three components of emotional intelligence (self-awareness, self-control, and intrinsic motivation) relate to skills for managing one's own behavior, while the last two, empathy and social skills, are linked to the ability to manage interactions with others.

This chapter explores how to use EI in everyday life, especially in the workplace and in daily interactions. Developing and applying emotional intelligence not only improves our relationships, but also helps us manage stress, increase satisfaction, and promote success in various areas.

WHY IS IT IMPORTANT TO APPLY EI IN DAILY LIFE?

Applying emotional intelligence in daily life allows us to:

- **Increase decision-making effectiveness:** EI helps us analyze and control emotions that could bias our decisions, allowing us to make more balanced and rational choices.

- **Improve professional performance and success:** Emotionally intelligent people excel at leadership, conflict resolution, and teamwork. These qualities are essential in any work environment.

- **Strengthen interpersonal relationships:** EI helps us build deeper and more fulfilling connections because it enables us to better understand and respond to others' emotions.

- **Manage stress and pressure:** Self-awareness and self-control are key elements of EI. These help us manage stress and remain calm in challenging situations.

- **Increase well-being and happiness:** An emotionally balanced life allows us to enjoy experiences more and maintain a positive attitude when facing challenges.

EI IN THE WORKPLACE

The workplace presents numerous challenges that test our emotional intelligence. Below are some ways EI can be an advantage in work situations.

Managing work stress. In high-pressure moments, EI helps us identify our stress levels and respond consciously. Techniques such as deep breathing, mindfulness, and conscious pauses help us regain calm and tackle tasks in an organized way.

Making sound decisions. Work decisions are often influenced by emotions such as fear of making mistakes or time pressure. Self-awareness helps us separate momentary emotions from facts and evaluate options more clearly.

Effective communication. EI allows us to communicate clearly, assertively, and empathetically, reducing misunderstandings and improving collaboration. Good communication involves not just conveying our ideas but also listening and understanding others, which strengthens workplace relationships.

Empathetic leadership. Emotionally intelligent leaders inspire and motivate their teams through understanding and support. This type of leadership applies empathy and active listening, helping to create a positive work environment and increase team commitment.

Conflict management. Conflicts are inevitable in any work environment. EI allows us to manage conflicts productively by addressing them respectfully and seeking solutions that benefit both parties. Avoiding impulsive responses and opting for clear, direct communication helps resolve conflicts without damaging relationships.

Teamwork. Emotional intelligence allows us to understand and respect coworkers' different perspectives, which fosters collaboration. An emotionally intelligent team leverages diverse ideas and works in a supportive, respectful environment.

EI IN PERSONAL LIFE

Emotional intelligence also has a significant impact on our personal relationships and well-being. Below are some examples of how EI applies in everyday life.

Managing daily emotions. Self-awareness allows us to identify our emotions and understand their causes, helping us avoid impulsive reactions. By recognizing what we feel, we can make more conscious and effective decisions.

Improving family and partner relationships. Empathy, active listening, and assertive communication are essential for maintaining healthy, satisfying relationships. Applying EI in our personal relationships helps avoid unnecessary conflicts and strengthen bonds with loved ones.

Setting boundaries. In daily life, EI helps us set clear boundaries to protect our emotional well-being. Being assertive about our boundaries prevents us from feeling overwhelmed and ensures more balanced relationships.

Managing stress and anxiety. Self-control and self-awareness allow us to manage stress and anxiety that can arise in everyday situations. Techniques such as mindful breathing, physical exercise, and prioritizing help us maintain a clear and focused mind.

Making personal decisions. EI helps us make decisions that align with our values and desires. By understanding our emotions and deeper needs, we make choices that bring us closer to a fulfilling and satisfying life.

STRATEGIES FOR APPLYING EI IN WORK AND DAILY LIFE

1. **Practice conscious pauses:** Before responding in a conversation or stressful situation, take a brief pause to reflect on what you're going to say or do. This technique is especially useful at work, where emotions can influence our response. The conscious pause allows us to respond calmly and clearly.

2. **Set clear and realistic goals:** Defining realistic goals helps us stay focused and prevents us from feeling overwhelmed. Setting goals, both in work and personal life, increases our motivation and allows us to measure our progress objectively.

3. **Practice self-care:** Emotional intelligence also involves taking care of ourselves. Healthy eating, regular exercise, proper rest, and time for leisure activities are essential to maintaining good emotional health.

4. **Improve self-awareness through journaling:** Keep a journal where you reflect on your emotions, thoughts, and daily experiences. Reviewing your entries helps identify emotional patterns and work on areas that need improvement.

5. **Use breathing and mindfulness techniques:** Conscious breathing and mindfulness are effective tools for reducing stress and increasing focus on the present moment. These practices help us manage our emotions more effectively and make decisions with a clear mind.

6. **Develop empathy in the workplace:** Empathy is a powerful skill at work. Take a moment to consider the perspective of your colleagues and acknowledge their emotions. This practice can significantly

improve the work environment and foster a culture of respect and understanding.

7. **Provide constructive feedback:** Practicing constructive feedback helps strengthen workplace relationships and improve team performance. Being clear and specific in feedback avoids misunderstandings and promotes continuous improvement.

8. **Use the power of gratitude:** Gratitude is a powerful tool for cultivating a positive mindset. Practice daily gratitude, whether by thanking colleagues at work or appreciating positive moments in daily life. This habit enhances emotional well-being and strengthens our relationships.

EXERCISES TO DEVELOP AND APPLY EI IN LIFE AND WORK

1. **Deep breathing exercise:** Practice deep breathing during stressful moments by inhaling deeply for four seconds, holding the breath for four seconds, and exhaling slowly for another four seconds. Repeat several times until you feel calm and ready to face the situation.

2. **Daily emotional reflection:** At the end of the day, reflect on your experiences and emotions. Identify situations that generate joy, frustration, anxiety, etc. and think about how you could improve your emotional response in similar situations in the future.

3. **Empathetic listening exercise:** During conversations, make a conscious effort to listen without interrupting and show that you value the other person's perspective. This exercise strengthens empathy and improves the quality of relationships.

4. **Prioritize and organize time:** Make a task list and organize your priorities. Setting an order helps reduce stress and increases productivity. By managing time effectively, you also have more space for self-care and relationships.

5. **Develop personal goals:** Define clear, realistic goals for both your personal life and career. Set an action plan and celebrate your achievements when you reach them. This exercise fosters motivation and personal growth.

CONCLUSION

Emotional intelligence is not just a theory; it is a daily practice that profoundly impacts the quality of our relationships, professional success, and personal well-being. People are generally more effective at managing relationships when they understand and manage their own emotions and can put themselves in others' shoes to understand their feelings. By applying EI at work and in daily life, we develop a fundamental skill that helps us face challenges with greater clarity and maintain strong, meaningful relationships. EI is the tool that helps us live a more balanced, fulfilling, and purposeful life.

NOTES:

CHAPTER 8: EMOTIONAL INTELLIGENCE AND PERSONAL WELL-BEING

"When emotional intelligence merges with spiritual intelligence, human nature is transformed."

DEEPAK CHOPRA

INTRODUCTION

Developing strong emotional intelligence can be key to improving our quality of life, increasing personal satisfaction, and cultivating greater resilience in the face of challenges. Having a high level of emotional intelligence promotes more effective adaptation to the environment, which in turn contributes to greater psychological well-being, and individuals with high emotional intelligence tend to have stronger self-esteem, better emotional control, and greater empathy, all of which positively impact their mental and emotional well-being.

Emotional intelligence (EI) not only influences our relationships and professional achievements but is also a fundamental pillar for our personal well-being. This chapter explores how EI contributes to emotional, mental, and physical well-being and provides practical strategies for applying it in our daily lives.

WHAT IS PERSONAL WELL-BEING?

Personal well-being encompasses various aspects of life, including physical, emotional, mental, and social well-being. Personal well-being is defined as a state in which a person experiences high levels of life satisfaction, shows few signs of emotional distress, and enjoys a general sense of happiness. It involves experiencing a sense of balance, contentment, and inner peace.

Unlike temporary happiness, well-being is a deeper, more stable state that is sustained over time. Personal well-being goes beyond happiness; it involves the holistic development of the individual in various areas of life. Emotional intelligence is key in this process because it allows us to manage our emotions in a healthy way, build meaningful relationships, and make decisions that support our personal growth and happiness.

HOW DOES EMOTIONAL INTELLIGENCE CONTRIBUTE TO PERSONAL WELL-BEING?

- **Emotional regulation:** EI allows us to recognize and manage our emotions consciously, avoiding impulsive reactions and minimizing the impact of negative emotions on our well-being. By regulating our emotions, we reduce stress and promote calmness.

- **Self-awareness and authenticity:** With greater self-awareness, we can understand what we truly want and need in life. This helps us live in alignment with our values, be authentic, and make decisions consistent with our true identity, thereby increasing our personal satisfaction.

- **Resilience and stress management:** Emotional intelligence helps us face difficulties with a positive and proactive mindset. Resilience is the ability to bounce back from challenges and learn from them, which is essential for maintaining strong emotional well-being over time.

- **Healthy relationships:** Emotionally intelligent individuals develop deeper, more meaningful relationships that provide support, joy, and a sense of belonging. These relationships contribute significantly to well-being, as they offer emotional support and reinforce our self-esteem.

- **Motivation and personal growth:** EI helps us stay motivated and committed to our personal goals. This internal motivation fosters a sense of purpose and direction in life, increasing our satisfaction and personal fulfillment.

KEY COMPONENTS OF PERSONAL WELL-BEING AND EI

Emotional well-being. Emotional well-being involves the ability to manage our emotions in a healthy way. Self-awareness and self-control are essential here, as they allow us to recognize our emotions and respond constructively.

Mental well-being. A calm and balanced mind greatly contributes to our well-being. EI helps reduce negative thoughts, improve focus, and maintain an optimistic perspective.

Physical well-being. Although seemingly disconnected from EI, physical well-being is directly related to our emotions. Emotionally intelligent individuals are more aware of their bodies and how physical care influences their emotions, leading them to adopt positive health habits.

Social well-being: The ability to establish and maintain meaningful relationships is key to social well-being. Empathy, active listening, and assertiveness are EI skills that enrich our relationships and help us build emotional support networks.

STRATEGIES TO IMPROVE PERSONAL WELL-BEING WITH EI

1. **Practice self-observation and self-awareness:** Take time to reflect on your thoughts and emotions. Keep a personal journal to record how you feel and what factors contribute to those feelings. This will help you identify patterns and become more aware of your emotional needs.

2. **Use emotional regulation techniques:** Emotional regulation is key to maintaining personal well-being. Techniques like deep breathing, meditation, and positive visualization are useful for calming the mind and reducing stress. You can also try the "reframing" technique, which involves shifting your focus from a negative emotion to an activity that brings you well-being.

3. **Cultivate a gratitude attitude:** Gratitude is a powerful tool for emotional well-being. Every day, write down three things you are grateful for. This practice increases positivity and reduces focus on negative thoughts, contributing to greater emotional well-being.

4. **Develop self-care habits:** Self-care is essential for maintaining a healthy balance between mind and body. Make sure to include activities you enjoy in your daily routine and that allow you to relax, such as reading, exercising, meditating, or engaging in a hobby.

5. **Foster resilience and a positive mindset:** Resilience helps you overcome obstacles without compromising your well-being. Practice "cognitive reframing," a technique that involves finding a positive

aspect in difficult situations, enabling you to maintain an optimistic perspective.

6. **Establish and maintain healthy relationships:** The quality of your relationships directly influences your well-being. Work on your communication skills, show empathy, and set healthy boundaries. Surround yourself with people who add value to your life and support your personal growth.

7. **Practice mindfulness:** Mindfulness helps you live in the present moment, reducing anxiety and stress. Spend a few minutes each day observing your thoughts and sensations without judgment. This practice increases self-awareness and reduces emotional reactivity.

8. **Set personal goals and acknowledge your achievements:** Having clear goals and working toward them provides a sense of purpose. Set realistic goals, and when you achieve them, take time to celebrate your successes. This process boosts motivation and self-confidence, strengthening your overall well-being.

EXERCISES TO IMPROVE PERSONAL WELL-BEING WITH EI

1. **Gratitude journal:** At the end of each day, write down three things you are grateful for. This exercise helps train your mind to focus on positive aspects, promoting a more balanced mood and an optimistic attitude.

2. **Practice conscious breathing:** When you feel overwhelmed or stressed, practice conscious breathing. Inhale deeply, count to four, hold the breath for four seconds, and exhale slowly. This exercise reduces stress and improves mental clarity.

3. **Weekly reflection exercise:** Every week, take time to reflect on your emotions, achievements, and challenges. Write in your journal what you learned and how you can improve for the following week. This practice fosters self-awareness and helps you adjust your actions to continuously improve your well-being.

4. **Positive visualization:** Spend a few minutes every morning visualizing a successful day. Imagine how you will face challenges calmly and how you will make the most of opportunities. This exercise prepares your mind to face the day with a positive attitude.

5. **Body scan meditation:** Practice body scan meditation to release physical tension. This practice involves closing your eyes, breathing deeply, and mentally scanning each part of your body, noticing any tension or discomfort, and allowing it to relax. Regular practice improves both physical and mental well-being.

6. **Personal achievement visualization exercise:** Close your eyes and imagine a future version of yourself who has achieved your personal goals and lives according to your values. Visualize how you feel, what you do, and how you behave. This practice motivates and strengthens your commitment to your goals.

HOW EI ENHANCES QUALITY OF LIFE

When we apply emotional intelligence in our lives, personal well-being becomes a tangible and sustainable reality. By developing a better understanding of our emotions and learning how to manage them, we build a strong foundation of self-confidence and satisfaction. Individuals with high emotional intelligence enjoy greater satisfaction in their personal lives, exhibit greater resilience, and manage their emotions better, all of which contribute positively to their well-being.

EI allows us to live in the present, enjoy our experiences, and maintain a positive perspective during difficult times. It helps us view problems as opportunities for learning and growth, increasing our resilience and ability to adapt to change.

CONCLUSION

Emotional intelligence is a powerful tool for achieving and maintaining personal well-being. By improving our self-awareness, emotional regulation, and empathy toward others, we build a richer, more fulfilling, and balanced life. Developing EI helps us find greater inner peace, build strong relationships, and face challenges with a positive attitude. Ultimately, solid emotional intelligence not only makes us happier and healthier, but also enables us to live a life with greater purpose and meaning.

NOTES:

CONCLUSION AND NEXT STEPS

"We know what we are,
but know not what we may be."

WILLIAM SHAKESPEARE

Emotional intelligence (EI) is a fundamental skill that profoundly influences all aspects of our lives. From self-awareness to managing interpersonal relationships, from regulating our emotions to facing challenges with resilience, EI significantly impacts our well-being and success. By developing emotional intelligence, we can improve our relationships, increase productivity, and approach challenges with a positive, balanced mindset.

Throughout this book, we have explored various dimensions of EI and how each one contributes to creating a more fulfilling life. We have learned to manage our emotions, improve communication, lead with empathy, and make more balanced and mindful decisions. However, EI is not a one-time achievement, rather an ongoing process that requires practice, patience, and commitment.

THE IMPORTANCE OF CONSTANT PRACTICE

The development of emotional intelligence doesn't happen overnight. It is a continuous process involving self-observation, introspection, and, above all, the willingness to improve. Developing emotional intelligence is not easy; it requires time, effort, and, most importantly, consistent commitment. Like any skill, EI improves with regular practice and the desire to grow. Each day presents new opportunities to apply what we have learned in our daily interactions at work, in managing stress, and in our personal relationships.

It is important to remember there is no "correct" way to be emotionally intelligent. Every person is unique, so the journey to developing EI will be different for each of us. What is universal, however, is the idea that by becoming more aware of our emotions and how they affect our decisions and relationships, we can live more fully and authentically.

NEXT STEPS

The following steps will allow you to continue developing your emotional intelligence and apply what you've learned in your daily life:

1. **Personal evaluation:** Take a moment to reflect on your own emotional intelligence. Which areas do you feel strongest in? Which areas could you improve? This will provide a foundation for focusing your future efforts.

2. **Set emotional goals:** As with any personal development process, it is helpful to set clear, achievable goals. You can start with simple goals, such as practicing empathy more often or learning to regulate your emotions in stressful situations.

3. **Practice daily techniques:** Integrate EI exercises and techniques into your daily routine. From meditation and conscious breathing to daily reflection or emotional journaling, these practices will help improve your self-awareness and manage your emotions more effectively.

4. **Seek feedback:** Talk to trusted friends, family, or colleagues about your progress. Sometimes others can see aspects of our emotional intelligence that we might not perceive ourselves. Constructive feedback is a valuable tool for personal growth.

5. **Start a continuous development plan:** EI is a continuous journey. Make a commitment to yourself to keep learning about emotional management, empathy, conflict resolution, and self-care. Reading books, attending seminars, or even seeking an emotional mentor or coach can be useful options for continuing to move forward.

6. **Cultivate patience and compassion:** It is essential to be patient with yourself throughout this process. Emotional intelligence, like any skill, takes time to develop. Practice self-compassion and remember every step forward is a victory.

7. **Apply EI in different contexts:** As you continue developing your EI, look for ways to apply it in various aspects of your life: at work, with your family, in your friendships, and in your relationship with yourself. By applying EI in diverse situations, you will learn to adapt and improve it in different contexts.

8. **Maintain a growth mindset:** Emotional intelligence has no end point. There is always something new to learn or an area to improve. Keep a growth mindset, ready to learn from your experiences and continue evolving.

EI AS A PATH TO SELF-KNOWLEDGE AND FULFILLMENT

Ultimately, emotional intelligence is not just about managing our emotions or improving our relationships. At its core, EI is a powerful tool for self-knowledge and self-fulfillment. It allows us to live more consciously, aligned with our deepest values and desires. By learning to manage our emotions and understand others, we get closer to a balanced, fulfilling, authentic life.

It is a continuous growth journey that transforms the way we live, relate to the world, and face the challenges that come our way. Keep exploring, learning, and practicing emotional intelligence in your daily life. The benefits of this process—both for yourself and others—will be profound and lasting.

Let your journey toward a more emotionally intelligent and fulfilling life begin!

NOTES:

REFERENCES

Andújar, C. A. (2004). Development and preliminary validation of the Emotional Intelligence Inventory in a sample of university students. Interamerican Journal of Occupational Psychology, 23(1), 38-55.

Asana. (2024, February 10). What is intrinsic motivation and how does it work? Asana. asana.com/es/resources/intrinsic-motivation

Bradberry, T., & Greaves, J. (2009). Emotional Intelligence 2.0. TalentSmart.

Diener, E. (1984). Subjective well-being. Psychological Bulletin, 95(3), 542-575. doi.org/10.1037/0033-2909.95.3.542

Freytes, S. (2004). Emotional intelligence and post-traumatic stress disorder in crime victims. Unpublished doctoral dissertation. Carlos Albizu University, San Juan, Puerto Rico.

Garaigordobil, M., & Peña, A. (2014). Intervention in social skills: Effects on emotional intelligence and social behavior. Behavioral Psychology/ Psicología Conductual, 22(3), 551-567.

Goleman, D. (1995). Emotional intelligence: Why it can matter more than IQ. Bantam Books.

Goleman, D. (1998). Working with emotional intelligence. Bantam Books.

Goleman, D. (2004, October). What makes a leader? Harvard Business Review Latin America.

Gudiña, V. (2024, May 23). Self-awareness: What it is, its importance, characteristics, and examples. Definición.de. definicion.de/autoconciencia/

García-Allen, J. (2016, June 12). Self-control: 7 psychological tips to improve it. Psychology and Mind Portal. psicologiaymente.com/psicologia/autocontrol-consejos

Muñoz Zapata, A. P., & Chaves Castaño, L. (2013). Empathy: A univocal concept? Katharsis, 16, 123-146 doi.org/10.25057/25005731.467

Palmer, B. (2003). An analysis of the relationship between various models and measures of emotional intelligence. Swinburne University of Technology.

Palmer, B., Gardner, L., & Stough, C. (2003). Measuring emotional intelligence in the workplace with the Swinburne University Emotional Intelligence Test. In Proceedings of the First International Conference on Contemporary Management (ICCM): Emotional Intelligence in Organizations.

Plutchik, R. (1980). Emotion: A psychoevolutionary synthesis. HarperCollins College Division.

Roca Villanueva, E. (2013). Emotional intelligence and related concepts: Healthy self-esteem and social skills. In Congress on Emotional Intelligence and Well-being (Zaragoza, 2013).

Ryff, C. D. (1989). Happiness is everything, or is it? Explorations on the meaning of psychological well-being. Journal of Personality and Social Psychology, 57(6), 1069-1081. doi.org/10.1037/0022-3514.57.6.1069

Salovey, P., & Mayer, J. D. (1990). Emotional intelligence. Imagination, Cognition, and Personality, 9(3), 185-211. doi.org/10.2190/DUGG-P24E-52WK-6CDG

ABOUT THE AUTHOR

Gisela M. Rentas, PhD, is a distinguished educator, psychologist, and child development specialist. She currently serves as the Education Manager and Coordinator at the Charleston County School District in South Carolina. Her focus is on the professional development of staff, continuous improvement of educational quality, and support for individualized child learning.

Dr. Rentas holds a Bachelor's in Psychology from the University of Puerto Rico, a dual Master's in Psychology and Early Childhood Education, and a Ph.D. in Industrial Organizational Psychology from the Interamerican University of Puerto Rico.

Dr. Rentas firmly believes emotional intelligence is the cornerstone of success and the foundation for a happy and fulfilling life. She has made significant contributions to the field, particularly through her research on emotional intelligence in managers within the government service industry in Puerto Rico.

In addition to writing, Dr. Rentas enjoys exercise and dance, especially classical ballet, which she has practiced for over ten years. She currently lives in Charleston, South Carolina with her husband of twenty-two years and their son.